Stop Being an NPC

How to Gamify Your Reality, Build an Empire, and Unlock Main Character Energy

John L. Hummel

Disclaimer:

This book is not a gentle self-help manual. The principles and strategies contained within are designed to fundamentally challenge your current reality and may necessitate difficult, life-altering decisions. The knowledge presented here is a set of "cheat codes" intended to help you hack your brain, unlock your full potential as a player, and level up out of the NPC role. Be warned: actively applying this material is for the bold, not the faint of heart. It is a catalyst for radical change and agency, not a guarantee of instant success, nor is it a comprehensive guide to being the best player, but rather a guide to starting your journey to becoming the main character in your own life.

First Edition: April 2026

ISBN: 978-1-9194834-0-5

Published by: JH Motiv LTD

London, United Kingdom

Dedication:

This is for the glitches.

For the people who look at the 9 to 5 script and sense that something is fundamentally wrong with the code. For those who are tired of being background assets in someone else's empire.

I dedicate this to everyone who has ever felt the crushing weight of being an NPC. Repeating the same actions, paralyzed by the fear of the unknown, watching the years render out without a save file to show for it.

May these pages serve as your exploit. May you find the courage to disconnect from the hive mind, rewrite your source code, and finally pick up the controller.

The simulation ends here. Your game begins now.

Table of Contents

Part I: The Glitch	Page 5 - 33
Chapter 1: The NPC Script	Page 5 - 17
Chapter 2: Picking Up the Controller	Page 18 - 24
Chapter 3: The Fog of War	Page 25 - 33
Part II: Character Creation	Page 34 - 54
Chapter 4: Assess Your Stats	Page 34 - 40
Chapter 5: Choose Your Character Class	Page 40 - 47
Chapter 6: Min-Maxing Your Life	Page 48 - 54
Part III: The Grind	Page 55 - 74
Chapter 7: Completing Your Dailies	Page 55 - 61
Chapter 8: Resource Management	Page 62 - 68
Chapter 9: The Tech Tree	Page 69 - 74
Part IV: Multi Player Mode	Page 75 - 94
Chapter 10: Building Your Guild	Page 75 - 81
Chapter 11: Don't Feed The Trolls	Page 82 - 87
Chapter 12: Understanding "The Meta"	Page 88 - 94
Part V: Endgame	Page 95 - 106
Chapter 13: The Boss Battle	Page 95 - 100
Chapter 14: New Game+	Page 101 - 106
Extras	Page 107-109
Appendix	Page 110 - 114
Further Debugging	Page 115+

___PART I: THE GLITCH___

Chapter 1: The NPC Script

Wake up. Put clothes on.

Grab a snack and an energy drink.

Commute.

This is the ritual. A Pavlovian response to the digital alarm, a pre-programmed sequence executed with the efficiency of a thousand previous iterations. You engage the ignition or step onto public transport with your eyes vacant, your attention already lost in the low-resolution texture of your phone screen. You are heading toward a destination you didn't choose, to perform a set of arbitrary tasks that hold no meaning for your personal narrative. You do this, not for fulfillment, but for a meager reward. A paycheck that barely covers the cost of keeping your physical avatar sustained enough to repeat the cycle tomorrow.

This is the Loop. This is the Script.

For approximately 250 working days a year, you run this identical program. You arrive at the corporate facility, the *instance*, where you execute the company's proprietary code. You communicate using the same six lines of carefully crafted, inoffensive dialogue, repeated in a thousand subtle variations just to maintain the illusion of unique thought and personal sanity. You deploy a mandated smile when a higher-level player, an *Admin*, enters the room. You nod in agreement to strategies and mission goals you neither understand nor care about. You are a resource generator: during your shift, you will produce £500, £1000, or more in gross profit for the company, and in return, they dispense minimum wage, or just a marginal amount more. It is a calculated allotment precisely enough *crumbs* to ensure your stamina bar does not hit zero, but critically, *never* enough to purchase your financial freedom, to buy the license for your own agency.

You clock out. The commute back is a blurry reverse image of the morning. You eat a quick, utilitarian meal. You sleep.

You run this script for ~50 weeks out of the year, existing in a state of perpetual supplication, praying that the Admins, your supervisors and managers will approve your request for a single week of personal time, your *holiday*. You are reduced to begging for the right to use your own life. Half the time, the request is denied. The official reason is always a logistical blocker: "we can't cover the shift," or "someone else got to the resource first." The functional reality is that you are an essential, low-level component, and the machine cannot tolerate your absence. You are trapped in legal limbo, a modern, corporate slave to a system that demands the full, irreversible expenditure of your life's finite resource *time* in exchange for the bare minimum of survival.

If you are reading this description and a familiar, cold dread is settling in your stomach if you are nodding your head in recognition then it is my painful duty to deliver the bad news. **You are not currently the Main Character of your life. You are an NPC**

The Definition of a Non-Player Character (NPC)

In the architecture of a video game, an NPC, or Non-Player Character, is a background entity, a piece of set dressing with a basic utility function. They possess no true agency or free will. They are rigidly programmed to walk a specific path (*pathing*) and utter specific lines of dialogue to serve the narrative, quest, or convenience of the *real* players. They exist to populate the world, to make it feel dense and active, rather than to genuinely change or influence it.

In the terrifying reality we inhabit, the definition is functionally identical: **Being an NPC is not a financial designation; it is a question of control and agency.**

It is irrelevant how large your bank balance is. The critical metric is: **Who holds the controller?**

If the allocation of your time, the source of your income, and the boundaries of your personal growth are dictated by someone else's code, the code of a corporation, a culture, or a societal expectation then you are merely running their script. You are not a human being with self-determination; you are an asset in someone else's inventory, a fungible resource.

This system, the game in which you are currently trapped, was written by individuals who have no skin in the game of *your* life. The intricate code that governs your trajectory, the rigid structure of the education system, the pyramidal corporate hierarchy, the suffocating blanket of societal expectations was all designed, written, and deployed by others. Their code promises security. It creates the illusion that if you just follow the prescribed pathing, if you stick religiously to the sidewalk, you will be safe, rewarded, and protected.

But look closely at the *texture* of that safety. It is a miserable, low-grade existence. It is the sinking feeling of being a number in a spreadsheet, a line item to be optimized and eventually culled. It is the crushing knowledge that the finish line keeps moving further away, regardless of how hard you try or how fast you run. The cost of living is *always* increasing, while the rewards for your loyalty, the meager annual bonus if any, and the cost of living get smaller with every passing *patch update*.

The Dialogue Wheel of the Damned

The most insidious part of the NPC script is not the external commands issued by your boss; it is the *internal monologue* the defensive scripts you run on yourself. Over decades of observing both the gaming world and the business world, I have noticed that human NPCs all default to self-limiting **Dialogue Wheel** phrases. These phrases are internal pathing blockers, psychological code designed to keep you comfortably and permanently inside the bubble of the status quo. The longer you stay in that bubble, the denser and more inescapable the atmosphere becomes.

Does this internal dialogue sound familiar?

- **"I can't afford to do that."** (The resource constraint.)

- **"I don't have time."** (The time constraint.)

- **"I'll do it tomorrow/next week/when I retire."** (The procrastination loop.)

- **"Must be nice to have a life like that."** (The externalization of agency.)

- **"I can't do that because I might fail/I'm not smart enough."** (The fear based constraint.)

These are not logical reasons; they are **pathing blockers**. When you observe a true player, someone living a fulfilled, unconventional life and your internal voice says, "must be nice," you are explicitly conceding your position as a spectator. You are watching a cinematic cutscene and simultaneously programming yourself with the belief that participation is not an option.

When you say, "I'll do it tomorrow," you are making a fatal assumption. You are relying on an invisible, future save file that is just as likely to be corrupted, lost, or simply never loaded.

The True Cost of Following the Script

I learned the devastating true cost of the NPC mindset not through philosophy, but through a brutal financial hit. I didn't just lose a paycheck; I lost the foundation of an empire.

Let's review the **Combat Log**.

In 2007, I survived a brutal car accident. The crash was physically and emotionally crippling, but it resulted in a settlement check of $50,000. This money was not a gift; it was a resource granted in exchange for serious physical damage taken. It was compensation.

Fast forward to 2010. A year that ironically became a permanent marker of my financial bondage.

I was staring at a new, volatile, and deeply exciting opportunity called Bitcoin. I had done the research and was ready to allocate $15,000 of that settlement money, roughly ~30% of my total stash, to bet on this new digital currency.

At that specific time, Bitcoin was a phantom asset, nowhere on the average person's radar. It was the Wild West of finance. The price was fluctuating wildly, often trading in the *pennies or less*. Let's apply a conservative estimate and say that if I had executed the trade, I would have acquired 300,000 Bitcoin at an average cost of $0.05 per coin.

But I didn't execute the trade. The script kicked in.

The NPCs around me, the well-meaning but fatally cautious family and friends, saw that $50,000 settlement not as capital to be deployed, but as a sacred **safety net**. They launched their defensive dialogue: *"Don't blow it."* *"You got hurt for that money, you have to keep it safe."* *"Just put it in a savings account where it's guaranteed."*

I listened sort of. I allowed someone else's fear, someone else's conservative, low-risk code, to overwrite my own agency and intuition. I kept my $15,000 "safe" in the bank for the time being.

Today, just over a decade later, Bitcoin trades in the tens of thousands. Let's use a conservative, standard market estimate of $95,000 per coin for the sake of calculation.

Let's run the definitive math on the decision to "be safe" and listen to the NPCs:

$$300{,}000 \times \$95{,}000$$

$$=$$

$28,500,000,000

Twenty-Eight

Billion Dollars!!!

That single, paralyzing moment of hesitation, motivated by the pursuit of safety, did not cost me a luxury car or a nice house. **It cost me the approximate Gross Domestic Product of a small country.** Even if the panic of holding such a volatile asset had forced me to sell 99% of my stack, retaining just a 1% residual position would still be worth hundreds of millions of dollars.

*I didn't just lose $15,000. **I lost a dynasty.***

And the $15,000 I 'saved to be responsible'? It didn't even survive the tutorial. Over the next two years, from 2010 to 2012, I drained the account on a girlfriend and the very friends and family who begged me not to invest. I burned the capital on short-term pleasures and social maintenance. The money didn't buy me freedom; it bought me two years of distractions for the people who kept me trapped in the loop.

This trauma burned a hole in my soul, but it unlocked a permanent, vital perk: **I realized that safety, as it is defined by the status quo, is the most expensive thing you can buy.**

The people who advised me had my best interest at heart. They genuinely didn't want me to lose my accident money. But their core programming is fundamentally different from the goal of a Main Character. **They are playing on a Pacifist Server, where the core goal is simply to survive until the inevitable Game Over screen.** You, the one who wants more, need to be playing on a **PVP (Player vs. Player) Server**, where the objective is to conquer, to build, and to dictate the terms of the game.

The Lie of Safety

The original programmers of this system, the architects of the corporate, political, and educational spheres, need you to believe that the NPC route is the **safe route**. They deploy powerful propaganda that asserts starting a business is "too risky," that chasing a self-directed dream is "irresponsible," and that deviating from the script is "dangerous."

This is the biggest, most damaging lie in the entire game.

Being an NPC is the single most dangerous playstyle that exists. You have zero defensive stats, no true armor, and no control over your fate.

- **If the company misses its financial targets,** you are the first line item to be eliminated, deleted via **redundancy**.

- **If you get sick or your performance dips,** you are immediately flagged for replacement of a low-cost, fungible asset.

- **If the economy crashes or a new technology emerges,** you, the non-essential cog, are the first to suffer the full weight of the consequence.

You are dedicating your entire, finite life resource to someone who views you as a single, adjustable line item on a P&L (Profit & Loss) sheet. You operate under the toxic assumption that *they* care about your interests. They demonstrably do not. If you stay in this NPC Loop for the prescribed 40 years, you will inevitably arrive at the Game

Over screen having never actually *played* the game of
your own life.

The finish line you are running toward the promise of a
golden retirement and security is a **hologram**. It moves
further away every single year. The only way to truly win is
to **stop running their race entirely.**

It's time to find the exploit. It's time to break the script.
It's time to pick up the controller and code your own
destiny.

SIDE QUEST: THE SOURCE CODE AUDIT

Quest Giver: The Awakened Self
Difficulty: Tutorial (Easy) but Painful
XP Reward: +100 Awareness, +1 Reality Check

Objective: You cannot hack a system you do not
understand. Before you can break the script, you must see
the code. For the next 24 hours, you are going to run a
diagnostic on your own life.

Mission Parameters:

1. Map The Loop (Time Audit) For one single day, track
every hour of your existence in a notebook or phone app.
Do not change your routine; just observe it. Label every
block of time with one of two tags:

- **[NPC MODE]:** Time sold to someone else (job),
  time spent on unconscious maintenance

(commuting, mindless scrolling, chores), or time spent escaping reality (binge-watching, numbing).

- **[MAIN CHARACTER MODE]:** Time spent building assets, learning new skills, exercising, or creating something that belongs to you.

The Pass Condition: At the end of the day, calculate your **NPC Ratio**. *(Total NPC Hours / Total Waking Hours) x 100.* If your score is over 80%, you are critically exposed to the "Game Over" screen.

2. Catch the Glitch (Dialogue Defense) Your internal defense system will try to stop you from doing this audit. It will use the **Dialogue Wheel of the Damned**.

- **The Task:** Catch yourself saying one of the forbidden phrases ("I don't have time," "I'll do it tomorrow," "I can't afford it").

- **The Counter-Attack:** When you hear the phrase, force a **hard rewrite**.

    - *Instead of "I don't have time," say:* **"It is not a priority."**

    - *Instead of "I can't afford it," say:* **"I have not earned the resources yet."**

    - *Instead of "I'll do it tomorrow," say:* **"I am choosing to lose a day of progress."**

3. The Inventory Check Open your banking app. Look at the last 5 transactions.

- Did these purchases upgrade your character?

- Or did they simply patch your stamina bar so you could run the NPC script again tomorrow?

Status Update: Once you have completed the audit, stare at the data. That fear you feel? That isn't fear. That is the system realizing you have found the controller.

[PRESS START TO CONTINUE]

Chapter 2: Picking Up the Controller

Most people think being an NPC means you are lazy. They are wrong. You can work yourself into an early grave and still be an NPC.

I know this because I lived it.

I used to work 60 to 80 hours a week. I ground my bones to dust for a paycheck. And for what? To buy the latest consoles and games. I worked six days a week just to afford the privilege of escaping into a virtual world for my one day off.

I was working double-time in the real world just to fund my dissociation from it.

I felt like Neo from The Matrix. I knew something was wrong. The world felt "acceptable" but it never felt right. But unlike Neo I didn't just take the red pill to wake up. I didn't just take the blue pill to stay asleep.

I swallowed both pills at the same time.

I decided to learn exactly how the machine worked while refusing to let it own my mind. I played the part. I nodded at the bosses. I followed the rules. But internally I was mapping the level. I was learning the physics of the reality I intended to conquer.

The Two Types of Success

To understand why you need to pick up the controller you need to understand the difference between NPC success and Player success.

I have tasted both.

The NPC High: Years ago I was working at a theme park on a college program. I was a model employee. I followed every script. I was so good at being a cog in the machine that I got a pseudo-promotion. I was the first college student ever cross-trained for two different attractions.

I felt good. I felt validated. I felt like the system was petting me on the head and calling me a good boy. But looking back it was hollow. I was just a slightly more useful tool in someone else's inventory.

The Player High:

Compare that to the first time I ran the Vault of Glass raid in Destiny 1

I wasn't an employee there. I was a leader. I pulled together a squad of five complete strangers plus myself. We had no boss. We had no salary. We had a single objective. We were racing for World First from the shadows.

We weren't streaming. We were grinding. We beat every famous streamer to Atheon, the giant robot raid boss. We figured out the mechanics while the rest of the world was still scratching their heads. We had him on his last legs ten times before the big names even got into the room.

We didn't finish first because of a logistics failure. Someone needed to sleep and we lost momentum. But that feeling? That rush of coordinating five other strangers to achieve the impossible? That was real power.

That was the Agency.

In the theme park I was given a task. In the Vault of Glass I created a mission.

That is the difference. NPCs wait for orders. Players create objectives.

The Cage of Education

So why do we default to the NPC mode? Why is it so hard to pick up the controller in real life?

Because the tutorial level was rigged.

The school system is a factory designed to create NPCs. It isolates us. It teaches us that asking for help is "cheating." In the real world if you don't know the answer you ask an expert or you look it up. In school if you look it up you fail.

They sit you in a row and tell you to memorize data you will never need. They teach you to fear failure. They teach you that there is only one right answer and it is the one in the back of the teacher's book.

They hand you a map and tell you not to explore the edges.

This creates a psychological cage. You grow up terrified to try anything new because you are afraid you won't know the answer. You are afraid of looking stupid. You are afraid of the "F" grade.

But real life isn't a test. It's an open-world RPG.

In a game if you die to a boss you don't quit. You respawn. You change your loadout. You try a different strategy. You look up a guide. You ask for help.

The system tricked you into thinking you are helpless. It told you that you need permission to succeed.

Input vs. Output

Picking up the controller means flipping your energy flow.

NPCs are consumption machines. They have high Input. They watch TV. They read news. They scroll social media. They eat what is advertised. They absorb the world.

Players are creation machines. They have high Output. They build things. They sell things. They organize teams. They stream the content that the NPCs watch.

When I was working 80 hours a week I was an Input machine. I was absorbing orders and consuming entertainment.

When I led that raid team I was an Output machine. I was generating strategy and leadership.

You need to stop asking "What should I do?" and start asking "What can I create?"

You need to realize that the fear holding you back is just programmed code from a school system that wants you to be a worker, not a winner.

The cage is locked but the door is made of paper. Your mind is the key.

Pick up the controller. Press Start.

SIDE QUEST: THE "HELLO WORLD" PROTOCOL

Quest Giver: The Developer (You)

Difficulty: Moderate (Requires overcoming the "Cringe" Debuff)

XP Reward: +50 Creativity, +100 Agency

Debuff Removed: Spectator Syndrome

Objective: You have spent years as an **Input Machine**. Today, you flip the switch. Your mission is to generate one piece of **Output** and release it into the wild.

Mission Parameters:

1. Identify Your Drain (The Input Source) Look at where you spend your "NPC Time."

- Do you watch 3 hours of YouTube?

- Do you play 4 hours of COD?

- Do you scroll TikTok until your eyes bleed?

- Do you read business books but never start a business?

2. The Flip (Create the Asset) You are no longer allowed to consume without paying a tax of creation. You must create one "Asset" based on your Input.

- *If you game:* Don't just play. Write a 100-word strategy guide for the level you just beat. Record a 30-second clip of a funny moment.

- *If you scroll:* Stitch a video with your opinion. Remix a meme.

- *If you read:* Summarize the chapter you just read into a tweet or a LinkedIn post.

- *If you watch:* Write a review.

3. The Boss Fight: The "Publish" Button This is where the "School Cage" programming kicks in. You will feel fear. You will think, *"This isn't good enough,"* or *"People will think I'm weird."* That is the **Fear of the 'F' Grade**.

- **The Mechanic:** You must hit Publish, Send, or Post.

- **The Constraint:** You are not allowed to edit it for more than 5 minutes.

- **The Goal:** It does not need to be good. It just needs to be *real*.

Victory Condition: Once the post is live, look at it. You just moved from the audience to the stage. The quality is irrelevant. The fact that you pressed the button proves you are holding the controller.

[PRESS START TO CONTINUE]

Chapter 3: The Fog of War

In strategy games the Fog of War is the blacked-out portion of the map. It represents the unknown. It is where the monsters are. It is where the enemy base is. It is scary because you cannot see what is coming.

Most people stay in the starting base because they are afraid of the Fog. They think the base is safe.

I am here to tell you that the base is on fire.

The "Safety" you are clinging to is an illusion. You think your job is a fortress. It isn't. It is a house of cards built on a fault line. I have seen the floor fall out from under people who did everything right.

The Softlock: The Sick Day Trap

I worked with a guy who followed the rules. He got sick. He was told not to come in. He did exactly what he was told.

Then the system glitched.

They fired him for having too many sick days. When he tried to fight it they told him he needed a doctor's note. But his private doctor wouldn't issue a note for sickness lasting less than a week.

He was trapped in a bureaucratic loop. A softlock.

The company told him that if he could get the impossible note they would rehire him. But there was a catch. No back pay for lost hours. No sick pay. And he would be on a disciplinary trigger where one more mistake would lead to a permanent ban.

He didn't break the rules. The rules were written to ensure he lost.

The High-Performance Punishment

Later I worked in a call center during the pandemic. I made it to an unofficial Subject Matter Expert role. I was in the top tier. My team was the highest performing unit on the floor.

In a video game if you perform well you get loot. In the corporate world if you perform well you get punished.

They pulled us from our high-performing team and moved us back to an old section. Three days later they disbanded the entire team and made us redundant.

It wasn't a request. It was a demand.

I was lucky because I saw the attack coming. I quit the day they announced the move. Their response? They threatened to sue me for leaving a temporary role.

Think about that. They were preparing to fire me and my team but when I tried to leave on my own terms they threatened legal PvP. My team was wiped out and replaced by new hires who were cheaper and easier to control.

Loyalty is a one-way street. You can be the best player on the server and the Admins will still ban you if it saves them five dollars.

The Job Market Raid Boss

The most dangerous Fog of War isn't starting a business. It is relying on the job market.

I was promoted from Team Lead to Manager in less than six months. Although logistical issues delayed my full transition into the Manager role, I achieved this promotion within an eight-month timeframe. I was winning. Then the company restructured and forgot about the managers. I stepped down to pivot my class. I wanted to be a Full Stack Developer.

I learned the code. I built the projects. I applied to thousands of roles.

Silence.

I got rejection emails saying "we are no longer hiring" only to see the same job posted two weeks later. It was a ghost ship. Nothing changed. I improved my CV. I leveled up my LinkedIn. I did the grind.

Six months later the entry-level roles were demanding 5 to 10 years of experience. They wanted a max-level character for a level 1 dungeon.

I watched the economy go into freefall. My "safe" day job slashed hours. We were doing the work of two people for near minimum wage. We were told to take our breaks at impossible times. We were forced to follow robotic scripts for KPIs.

We became replaceable parts in a machine that was breaking down.

They forget that business isn't a hierarchy. It is a chain. We are the links. If you neglect the links the chain breaks. But they don't care. They will run you into the ground to stay afloat for one more quarter.

It is me today. It could be you tomorrow.

The Second Leap of Faith

I realized that waiting for the Fog to clear was a death sentence. I had to walk into it.

In April 2025 I made a jump. I started a streetwear brand.

I didn't have venture capital. I didn't have a rich dad. I did it with as little money as possible to prove a point. I wanted to show that the organic method works. It is slow. It grinds. But it compounds.

I realized that if I threw money at ads I could force success but that is "pay to win." I wanted to play the game on Hard Mode so I could learn the mechanics.

Then in September I unlocked a new class: **The Coach**.

I realized I had been doing this for over ten years. I had helped hundreds of coworkers get to 6-8 figure earnings. I was the grounding force that kept them going when they wanted to quit. They succeeded and moved on. Some forgot me. That is fine. Their success was my proof of concept.

I realized my value wasn't in following the script. It was in rewriting it for others.

The Stealth Grind

People will tell you it is impossible. They will tell you that you are wasting your time.

Look at MrBeast.

Before he was the biggest YouTuber on the planet, he was a kid in his mom's house. He pretended to go to college. He would drive to the campus and sit in his car to edit videos. He was effectively running a stealth mission: maintaining the disguise of a "Normal NPC" to keep his parents happy, while secretly grinding his real stats in the car park.

He struggled to get the money for his first big video. He gave a homeless man $10,000. It was everything he had.

Now he runs a game show empire. He helps hundreds of people. He found his purpose in what he loved and he monetized it.

He didn't wait for permission. He didn't wait for a degree. He unlocked his brain and stopped doubting his stats.

Walking Into the Fog

You have skills you are underestimating. Your day job taught you customer service. It taught you crisis management. It taught you how to deal with toxic players.

When I started this journey everyone doubted me. Some still do. But some have seen the dedication and are changing their tone.

I don't need their approval. I just need to keep moving one tile at a time into the Fog.

I still work a day job to fund the dream. I keep a roof over my head and food on the table. There is no shame in that. That is resource management.

But my mind is no longer in the cage. I am exploring the map.

This book is the map I have drawn for you. It isn't black and white. It isn't a list of "do this, do that." It is a blueprint to hack your mindset.

Stop seeking validation from the NPCs in your life. They are programmed to keep you safe in the base. But the base is burning.

The only safe place is out there is in the Fog.

SIDE QUEST: OPERATION SCOUT THE FOG

Quest Giver: Your Future Self
Difficulty: Hard (Requires facing financial anxiety)
XP Reward: +200 Vision, +50 Strategic Planning
Unlock: The "Exit Strategy" Blueprint

Objective: The Base is on fire, but you cannot run blindly into the dark. In strategy games, before you move your army, you send a Scout unit to reveal the map. Today, you are going to scout your escape.

Mission Parameters:

1. The "Game Over" Calculation (Stress Test the Base)
You believe your job is safe. Let's test that physics engine.

- Open your bank account.

- Look at your monthly "Burn Rate" (Rent or Mortgage + Food + Bills).

- **The Math: Total Savings / Monthly Burn Rate = Days of Survival.**

- *The Reality Check:* If your boss fires you today, exactly how many days until you hit 0 HP?

  - If the answer is less than 90 days, you are not "safe." You are standing on a trapdoor. Acknowledge this.

2. Identify Your "Car Park" (The Stealth Grind) MrBeast had his car. Where is your stealth zone? You cannot quit your job yet (Resource Management), so you must find a time-slot to build your new character while the Admins aren't looking.

- Is it 5:00 AM to 7:00 AM?

- Is it your lunch break in the car?

- Is it 9:00 PM to 11:00 PM after the kids sleep?

- **Action:** Block out one hour tomorrow. This is now a "Forbidden Zone." No Netflix. No scrolling. Only building.

3. Reveal One Tile of the Map The Fog is scary because you think there is nothing out there.

- **The Task:** Find one person who is currently making a full-time living doing the specific thing you want to do (e.g., selling streetwear, coding, coaching).

- **The Audit:** Do not look at their success. Look at their *start*. Scroll back to their first post. Look at their first product.

- **The Realization:** They are not special. They just walked into the fog 5 years before you did.

Status Update: Write down this sentence and tape it to your monitor/mirror: *"My job is not my life. It is just the investor funding my startup."*

[PRESS START TO CONTINUE]

PART II: CHARACTER CREATION

Chapter 4: Assess Your Stats

Society tells you that video games are a waste of time. They tell you that the thousands of hours you spent in Azeroth, Gielinor, or Los Santos were just "entertainment."

They are wrong.

If you have been gaming seriously for years you haven't just been playing. You have been training. You have been running simulations. You have been building a skill set that *(if translated correctly)* is worth millions in the real world.

It is time to audit your character. We need to look at the skills you *think* are useless and reveal them for what they actually are: High-level business stats.

Stat 1: Efficiency (The Speedrunner)

If you are used to grinding out skills in a game you inevitably learn how to optimize. You don't just kill mobs randomly. You find the best route. You stack buffs. You calculate exactly how much XP per hour you are getting.

In the corporate world this is called **SOPs (Standard Operating Procedures).**

Gamers are allergic to inefficiency. If a dungeon run takes 20 minutes but could take 15 we get annoyed. We fix the route. We optimize the loadout.

In business this is the difference between profit and bankruptcy. I realized that my obsession with "min-maxing" my character was actually an obsession with **Maximizing ROI (Return on Investment)**.

When I set up my business I didn't just guess. I built a system. I treated my daily workflow like a speedrun strategy. If a task didn't yield XP (profit) or loot (assets), I cut it from the rotation.

Stat 2: Economics (The Auction House Baron)

If you are like me you have probably controlled an entire server's economy as a solo player or with a small group. You bought low, sold high, and cornered the market on specific resources.

You understand **Supply and Demand** better than most economics graduates.

You know that if a new raid drops, the price of potions goes up. That is **Market Analysis**. You know that if you flood the market with copper ore, the price crashes. That is **Margin Protection**.

In real life business works exactly the same way. You need to understand what makes the economy tick.

Think about crafting. In a game, if you want to make a high-level armor piece you have two choices:

1. **Grind the mats yourself:** This costs zero gold but takes ten hours. (High Time Cost, High Margin).

2. **Buy the mats:** This costs gold but takes zero time. (High Cash Cost, Lower Margin).

This is the fundamental dilemma of every startup. Do you "grind the mats" (do the work yourself to save money) or do you "buy the mats" (outsource to save time)?

A gamer knows instinctively when to grind and when to buy. A gamer knows that time is a currency just as valuable as gold.

Stat 3: Problem Solving (The Raid Leader)

There are two ways to approach a new game or a business.

The Blind Run: You go in with zero knowledge. You learn to solve problems on the fly. You wipe. You adapt. You try again. This is the **Agile Startup** method. You build the plane while flying it.

The Walkthrough: You watch videos. You read the guides. You plan every aspect of your run before you press start. This is the **Business Plan** method.

Most successful businesses are a hybrid of both. You read the walkthrough (market research), but you accept that no run is identical. The RNG (luck/randomness) of real life will throw curveballs at you.

And what happens when you hit a wall? What happens in a challenging dungeon?

You don't quit. You communicate.

If you have ever led a raid you have learned **Management**. You learned how to assign roles (Tank, DPS, Healer). You learned that you can't do it all yourself. You learned that if the Healer dies, the party wipes.

In business, if your Operations Manager (Healer) quits, your Sales Team (DPS) will eventually die because they can't fulfill the orders. You have already learned team dynamics in the hardest environment possible: a voice chat with 20 frustrated strangers.

Stat 4: The Grind (The 99 Skill Cape)

This is the most important stat of all. **Resilience.**

Anyone who has ground a skill to Level 99 in RuneScape understands pain. You have to click the same tree, burn the same log, or catch the same fish tens of thousands of times. It is boring. It is repetitive. It is mind-numbing.

But you did it. Why?

Because you wanted the Cape. You wanted the payoff. You understood **Delayed Gratification**.

Real business is not a montage of excitement. It is boring. It is sending cold emails. It is debugging code. It is packing boxes. It is clicking the tree over and over again.

Most "normal" people quit when it gets boring. Gamers don't. We know that the grind is the price of the loot. We know that to get the achievement we have to push through the pain and suffering of the repetitive tasks.

If you can grind for a virtual cape you can grind for a real paycheck.

SIDE QUEST: THE STAT SHEET TRANSLATION

Quest Giver: The Game Master
Difficulty: High (Requires deep introspection)
XP Reward: +150 Self-Awareness, +1 Unique Class Ability
Unlock: The "Monetization" Skill Tree

Objective: You have been grinding skills for years. Whether in a video game, a dead-end job, or just managing your household. These are not "chores"; they are unallocated skill points. You must extract that XP and apply it to your new character.

Mission Parameters:

1. Build the Translation Matrix Grab a blank sheet of paper. Create three columns. You must fill in at least **three**

rows using skills from your gaming history OR your current job.

- **Column 1: The Source Mechanic (What you actually do)**
    - *Gaming Example:* Leading 40-man Raids, Theorycrafting builds.
    - *Day Job Example:* Handling screaming customers at a call center, Organizing shift rotas, Training new hires.
- **Column 2: The High-Level Stat (The Corporate Translation)**
    - *Translation:* Crisis Management, Operations Logistics, Team Leadership, Data Analysis.
- **Column 3: The Monetization (Who pays for this?)**
    - *The Target:* Freelance Consultant, Customer Success Manager for a Tech Startup, Corporate Trainer, eCommerce Operator.

2. System Warning: Accept the Lonely Road Before you proceed, you must acknowledge the Terms of Service for this new server.

- **The Warning:** By identifying these skills as *yours* (not your boss's), you are stepping off the designated path. There is no HR department here.

There is no Admin to restore your items if you get scammed. There is no safety net.

- **The Commitment:** Look at your list. Say out loud: *"I accept that I am now the Admin of my own life."*

3. Guild Recruitment (Ping the New Server) Because the road is lonely, you cannot survive with your old party members who are still stuck in the NPC loop. They will drag you back.

- **The Task:** Find **one** online community (Discord, Subreddit, Facebook Group, or Skool) where people are already playing this class.

- **Action:** Join. You don't have to post yet. Just enter the tavern, sit in the corner, and observe. Prove to your brain that there are other players on this server.

Status Update: Stop telling yourself you have no skills. You have the stats. You just need to equip the weapon.

[PRESS START TO CONTINUE]

Chapter 5: Choose Your Class

In the World of Warcraft Legion expansion I played a Druid.

If you know you know. It was the golden age of the Hybrid class. I wasn't just a tree healing the party. I was a bear taking the heavy hits. I was a cat shredding damage meters. I could do everything. I was a one-man army.

In the business world this is called being a Solopreneur.

When you first wake up from the NPC slumber you don't get the luxury of picking just one role. You don't have the budget to hire a Tank like a lawyer or a DPS like a sales guy. You are the Tank. You are the DPS. You are the Healer. You are the Crafter.

You are the Druid.

But here is the truth that most business books won't tell you. Multiclassing is a survival strategy. It is not an endgame build.

To build an empire you need to understand the four Archetypes. You need to know which one is your Main Spec which is your natural talent and which ones are your Off Specs which are skills you learned just to survive.

Most importantly you need to know when to stop shapeshifting and start recruiting.

The Four Archetypes of Business

Let's break down the real-world classes. You likely have skill points in all of them but one of these is your native tongue.

1. The Tank (The Shield & Structure) In gaming the Tank absorbs damage and controls aggro. They are hard to kill. In business this is Operations, Finance, and Risk Management. The Tank reads the terms and conditions. The Tank saves money just in case. They don't care about being the star. They care about the guild not disbanding. Their superpower is not panicking when the market crashes.

2. The DPS (The Sword & Growth) In gaming the Damage Dealer has fast twitch reflexes and wants to top the meters. They are Glass Cannons. In business this is Sales, Marketing, and Promotion. The DPS loves the hunt. They love the notification of a new sale on their phone. They are aggressive and loud. They generate the resource (Money) that keeps the rest of the party alive.

3. The Healer (The Spirit & Support) In gaming the Healer keeps the party alive and buffs teammates. In business this is Customer Service, HR, Coaching, and Community Management. The Healer cares about people. They notice when someone is burnt out. They turn a 1-star review into a 5-star fan. Their superpower is retention.

They know it costs more mana to get a new customer than to keep an old one.

4. The Crafter (The Hands & Product) In gaming the Crafter stays in the city and grinds materials to create items. In business this is Product Development, Coding, and Manufacturing. The Crafter is a builder. They can spend 12 hours alone working on a detail nobody else will notice. They often hate selling but they love making. Without them the DPS has nothing to sell.

The Druid Problem

Can you do all four of these? Yes. Can you do all four of these at the same time effectively? Only in short bursts.

In the game if you tried to Tank the boss and Heal the party and DPS the add's all at once you ran out of Mana. Your Actions Per Minute or APM had to be god-tier.

In real life your APM is your Mental Energy.

When I started my streetwear brand I was a Druid. I was the Crafter designing the shirts in the morning. I was the DPS posting TikToks in the afternoon. I was the Healer answering emails about everything in the evening. I was the Tank managing cash flow to buy the next batch of stock at night.

I was successful because I could multiclass. But I was exhausted. I knew I couldn't scale if I stayed in every form forever.

SIDE QUEST: THE CLASS SELECTION SCREEN

Quest Giver: The Guild Master

Difficulty: Moderate (Requires swallowing your pride)

XP Reward: +100 Self-Knowledge, +1 Strategic Hiring Roadmap

Unlock: The "Party Finder" Tool

Objective: You cannot multiclass forever. To scale, you must identify your "Main Spec" (what you are built for) and your "Dump Stat" (what kills you).

Mission Parameters:

1. Draw the Spec Sheet Take a piece of paper. Draw a large cross to create four quadrants. Label them:

- **Top Left: TANK** (Operations, Finance, Logistics). *Vibe: Safety & Order.*

- **Top Right: DPS** (Sales, Marketing, Pitching). *Vibe: Growth & Numbers.*

- **Bottom Left: HEALER** (Customer Support, HR, Culture). *Vibe: People & Service.*

- **Bottom Right: CRAFTER** (Product, Coding, Creating). *Vibe: Building & Deep Work.*

2. Assign Your Skill Points Be honest. You are not allowed to be good at everything.

- **Circle your Main Spec (Green Zone):** The tasks that give you energy. The work you would do for free.

- **Cross out your Dump Stat (Red Zone):** The tasks that make you want to rage-quit. The work you procrastinate on for weeks.

3. Read Your Combat Log (The Diagnosis) Find your combination below to reveal your fatal flaw and your required fix:

- **MAIN SPEC: TANK (The Organizer)**

  - *Red Zone is DPS?*
    You are The Library Keeper. Perfect systems, zero income.
    Fix: Hire a loud Sales Rep.

  - *Red Zone is Crafter?*
    You are The Middleman. All business, no product.
    Fix: Partner with a Developer/Creative.

  - *Red Zone is Healer?*
    You are The Robot. Efficient but cold. High churn.
    Fix: Hire a Community Manager.

- **MAIN SPEC: DPS (The Seller)**

  - *Red Zone is Tank?*

    You are The Gambler. High revenue, zero profit.

    Fix: Hire a strict Accountant/Ops Manager.

  - *Red Zone is Crafter?*

    You are The Hype Man. Great pitch, weak product.

    Fix: Stop selling, fix the product (or hire a dev).

  - *Red Zone is Healer?*

    You are The Wolf. You close deals but burn bridges.

    Fix: Hire an Account Manager to nurture clients.

- **MAIN SPEC: HEALER (The Helper)**

  - *Red Zone is DPS?*

    You are The Charity. High value, broke bank account.

    Fix: Hire a Closer to ask for the money.

  - *Red Zone is Tank?*

    You are The Martyr. You help everyone but forget to invoice.

    Fix: Automate billing or hire a VA.

- *Red Zone is Crafter?*

  You are The Consultant. Good advice, no assets.

  Fix: Hire a Ghostwriter/Dev to productize your brain.

- **MAIN SPEC: CRAFTER (The Builder)**

  - *Red Zone is DPS?*

    You are The Starving Artist. Beautiful product, invisible brand.

    Fix: Partner with a Marketer (50% equity) or learn to sell.

  - *Red Zone is Tank?* **You are The Chaos Creator.** Brilliant bursts, messy logistics. **Fix:** Hire a Project Manager.

  - *Red Zone is Healer?* **You are The Hermit.** Great code, ignores user feedback. **Fix:** Hire a Support Agent to buffer the humans.

4. Post the LFG (Looking For Group) Look at your **Red Zone**. You are no longer allowed to try and "get better" at this. You must outsource it. Write down the specific role you need to hire first. That is your next quest objective.

[PRESS START TO CONTINUE]

Chapter 6: Min-Maxing Your Life

In high-level gaming, the first thing a Pro Player does is adjust their settings. They turn down the graphics to get higher frames per second (FPS). They strip the UI (User Interface) to show only critical information. They set up Macros to automate complex button presses.

They Min-Max. They minimize the friction and maximize the output.

Most people play the game of life on "Default Settings." They have 200 ping. Their screen is cluttered with social media notifications. They are clicking abilities manually instead of using shortcuts.

If you want to run a business as a solo player (The Druid), you cannot afford to play on default settings. You need to optimize your UI.

Gear Slot 1: The Ultimate Macro (AI)

In MMOs, a "Macro" is a script that lets you press one button to perform five actions instantly. It is legal automation.

In the real world, this is **Artificial Intelligence.**

The single most useful "Best in Slot" item I have equipped isn't a physical object. It's AI.

As a business owner wearing every hat (*Tank, DPS, Healer, Crafter*) I don't have enough hours in the day to grind everything manually. I use AI to turn 8-hour tasks into 10-minute tasks.

- **Writing or copying?** Macro it with AI.

- **Debugging code?** Macro it with AI.

- **Drafting emails?** Macro it with AI.

This allows me to complete 80% of the grunt work in a fraction of the time. It prevents the stamina drain of switching roles constantly.

The Warning Label: AI is a tool, not a replacement player. You still need to steer the ship. You need to watch out for IP (Intellectual Property) issues and use it at your own discretion. But refusing to use AI today is like refusing to use "Add-ons" in World of Warcraft. You can play without them, but you will be out-performed by everyone who has them installed.

Gear Slot 2: Cooldown Management
(The Laundry Method)

Efficiency isn't about doing more things at once; it's about stacking your cooldowns correctly.

I structure my day by understanding my body's energy bar. I know when I have high mana (focus) and low mana.

I use a technique I call **"Active vs. Passive Cooldowns."**

- **Passive Cooldowns:** Tasks that take time to complete but don't require your presence. (e.g., Laundry, compiling code, rendering video, uploading files).

- **Active Cooldowns:** Tasks that require 100% of your input. (e.g., Coding, writing, sales calls).

I will start the laundry (Passive). While that machine is running for 60 minutes, I enter "Hackathon Mode" and code (Active). Then, I take a 10-minute break to hang the laundry.

I have completed two tasks in the same time block. Most NPCs do the laundry, wait for it to finish while scrolling their phone, and then try to work. They waste the cooldown window.

Gear Slot 3: The Priority System (The 1-5 Scale)

You cannot aggro every mob in the dungeon at once. You will wipe. You need a kill order.

I assign an invisible priority level to every task:

- **Level 5 (Boss Mechanic):** Immediate attention required. If I don't do this, we die (or lose money).

- **Level 1 (Trash Mob):** Not a priority. Can be ignored or saved for later.

I knock off one task at a time based on this level. If I get stuck on a Level 3 task (*if I hit a "Lag Spike" where I just can't solve the problem*) I don't sit there for three hours staring at the screen.

I move on.

If the game is lagging, you don't keep running into the wall. You go do a different quest. Control what is in your control.

The Environment: Organized Chaos

You will read a lot of books that tell you your desk must be sterile. They tell you that a clean desk equals a clean mind.

That is their build, not mine.

My workspace is an organized mess of chaos. I flourish in it. My "UI" looks messy to others, but I know exactly where every icon is.

You don't need a Pinterest-perfect setup. You need a setup where *you* flourish. If you need to spend 10 minutes resetting your environment to get in the zone, do it. But don't let "cleaning" become a procrastination mechanic.

The Hackathon Buff

When it is time to do the Level 5 tasks, I disconnect.

Social media is "Screen Clutter." It lowers your FPS. You cannot code complex architecture or write a book if you are checking Instagram every 4 minutes. That is like trying to raid while typing in general chat.

I go into **Hackathon Mode**. No socials. No notifications. Just the objective.

SIDE QUEST:
THE UI OPTIMIZATION PROTOCOL

Quest Giver: The Speedrunner
Difficulty: Easy (Instant Gratification)
XP Reward: +50 Efficiency, +100 Focus (FPS)
Unlock: The "Flow State" Buff

Objective: You are running life on "Default Settings," and your frame rate is dropping. It is time to open the Settings Menu, strip away the bloat, and configure your HUD for maximum performance.

Mission Parameters:

1. Configure Macros (AI Integration) Look at your work log from last week. Find the "Grind Task"—the thing that took 4+ hours and bored you to tears.

- **The Audit:** Is this task text-based or logic-based?

- **The Macro:** Open ChatGPT, Claude, or your AI tool of choice. Spend 15 minutes writing a prompt that does the first 80% of that task for you.

- **The Save:** Save that prompt. You just automated a daily quest.

2. Stack Your Cooldowns (The Laundry Protocol)
Identify a "Passive" task you need to do today (e.g., rendering video, compiling code, uploading large files, or literally doing laundry).

- **The Mistake:** Staring at the progress bar (Lag).

- **The Fix:** Trigger the Passive task immediately. While it buffers, sprint through a high-focus "Active" task. Do not stop until the Passive task pings "Complete."

3. Boost Your FPS (Clear the HUD) Your attention span is lagging because your screen is cluttered.

- **The Action:** Pick up your phone. Turn off **all** non-essential notifications (Socials, News, Email).

- **The Test:** Put the phone in "Airplane Mode" or "Focus Mode" for the next 60 minutes. Watch how much faster your brain renders the work.

4. The Physics Check (Accept the Chaos) Look at your physical workspace. Is it messy?

- **If Yes:** Does the mess physically prevent you from typing or working?

    - *If No:* **Ignore it.** Cleaning is often a procrastination mechanic.

- **The Momentum Rule:** If you hit an invisible wall on a specific task (Writer's Block/Bug), do not stand there running into the wall.

  - *Action:* Skip the mob. Go do a different task. Keep the character moving.

Status Update: Your settings are optimized. The lag is gone. Now, play the game.

[PRESS START TO CONTINUE]

PART III: THE GRIND

Chapter 7: Completing Your Dailies

In every MMO there is a mechanic known as "Dailies."

These are the repeatable quests that reset every morning. Go kill 10 boars. Collect 5 herbs. Craft 3 items. They are not glamorous. They are not the final boss fight. Most players hate them because they feel repetitive.

But the top players? The ones with the best gear and the most gold? They complete their Dailies every single time.

They know that consistency beats intensity.

If you want to be a Solopreneur you need to stop looking for the "one big break" and start falling in love with the daily rotation.

The Ideal Server Rotation

As a coach and a streetwear brand owner my days are not filled with yacht parties. They are filled with structure. I have designed a schedule that balances my Health Stats (Gym), my Wealth Stats (Work), and my Sanity Stats (Family).

This is my "Ideal Day" log.

07:30 - 08:30: Server Login (Wake Up & Fuel) I wake up and eat. This is the boot-up sequence. No checking emails in bed. Just fueling the engine.

08:30 - 10:45: Buffing Stats (The Gym) This is non-negotiable. Two hours of physical training. Most people think this is a waste of "work time." They are wrong. This is where I build the stamina required to handle the stress of business. If my physical health bar is low my mental focus drops. I am not just building muscle. I am building discipline.

11:00 - 12:30: Trade Skills (Fulfillment & Coaching) I enter the workspace. I switched hats to the "Tank" and "Healer." I handle Print on Demand orders. I handle custom orders for the streetwear brand. I do coaching calls. This is the grind. This is where the gold is actually farmed.

12:30 - 13:15: Consumables (Lunch) Refuel. Reset.

13:15 - 18:00: Main Quest Progression This is the deep work block. I am fulfilling more orders. I am working on the business strategy. I am handling the "Level 5" priority tasks we talked about in the last chapter. This is five hours of focused output.

18:00 - 21:00: Log Off (Family Time) The work stops. I switch to "Dad Mode" or "Partner Mode." This is crucial.

You cannot grind 24/7 without your character glitching out. I spend time with my family. I eat dinner. I disconnect from the matrix.

21:00 - 07:30: Offline Mode (Sleep) Rest recovery.

The Weekend Mechanic: Rested XP

In World of Warcraft if you log out in an inn or a city you gain "Rested XP." This means when you log back in you earn experience at double the rate.

My weekends are my Rested XP.

Saturday and Sunday are for family only. Sometimes I might do a tiny bit of work if there is a crisis but 95% of the time I am offline. This prevents burnout. It reminds me why I am grinding Monday through Friday. I am not building a business just to watch numbers go up. I am building it to have a life with the people I care about.

Consistency vs. Intensity

The biggest mistake NPCs make when they try to start a business is they try to sprint a marathon.

They work 16 hours a day for three days straight. They ignore their sleep. They skip the gym. They ignore their family. By Thursday they are exhausted. By Friday they quit.

That is "Intensity." Intensity fails.

"Consistency" is showing up from 11:00 to 18:00 every single day. It is doing the Print on Demand orders even when you don't feel like it. It is going to the gym even when it's raining.

The player who plays for 4 hours every day will always beat the player who plays for 20 hours once a month.

Dealing with RNG (Random Number Generation)

Now I called this my "Ideal" day for a reason. Real life has RNG.

Sometimes the kids get sick. Sometimes a supplier loses a shipment. Sometimes a coaching client has a crisis at 8 PM.

The schedule is a baseline. It is the target. If I hit this routine 80% of the time I win. If I miss a day I don't rage quit. I just respawn the next morning at 07:30 and start the rotation again.

Your Dailies are not optional. They are the price of admission for the life you want.

Your Mission: Program Your Server Rotation

You cannot copy-paste my build. My schedule works for my level, my class, and my family situation. You need to design a rotation that works for *your* current reality.

If you are currently working a 9-5 job and building your side hustle in the evenings, your rotation will look different. That is fine. The goal is intentionality, not freedom (yet).

SIDE QUEST:
PROGRAMMING THE SERVER ROTATION

Quest Giver: The Server Architect **Difficulty:** Endurance Test (Requires Consistency over Intensity) **XP Reward:** +100 Stamina, +50 Discipline **Unlock:** The "Routine" Perk (Reduces Decision Fatigue)

Objective: You cannot rely on willpower. Willpower is a mana bar that drains. You need a **Script**. Your mission is to hard-code a daily schedule that automates your success so you don't have to think about it.

Mission Parameters:

1. Define Server Uptime (Boundaries) A server cannot run at 100% capacity forever. It will overheat. You must set hard caps.

- **Login Time:** (When do you wake up?)

- **Log Off Time:** (When do you guarantee the laptop closes?)

- *The Rule:* Working past Log Off time is not "hustling." It is "system failure." It borrows energy from tomorrow. Respect the cap.

2. Apply Pre-Combat Buffs (Maintenance) Before you start the grind, you must buff your stats.

- **Physical Buff:** Gym, running, walking. (Minimum 30 mins).

- **Mental Buff:** Reading, meditation, or silence.

- *The Slot:* Schedule this **before** you check email. Do not enter combat unbuffed.

3. The Raid Window (Main Quest) This is your Deep Work block. This is where you generate the gold (Sales, Coding, Creating).

- **Time Block:** Aim for 2-4 hours.

- **The Firewall:** No email. No social media. No Discord. If it's not the Main Quest, it is blocked.

4. Inventory Management (Admin Batching) These are the "Trash Mobs"—emails, shipping, invoices. They are annoying but necessary.

- **The Strategy:** Do not let them roam free. Cage them into a specific time block.

- **Time Block:** (e.g., 1 hour before Lunch OR 1 hour before Log Off).

5. Lag Compensation (RNG Buffer) Real life has lag. Traffic is bad. The kids are sick. A client is angry.

- **The Fix:** Leave **30-60 minutes completely empty** in your schedule.
  - *Scenario A (Smooth Run):* Use it for extra work or rest.
  - *Scenario B (Glitch):* Use this time to fix the crisis without ruining the rest of your day.

Victory Condition: Write this rotation down physically. Stick it to your wall. **Run this script for 7 days.**

- *If you succeed:* Keep running it.
- *If you fail:* Check the logs. Did you set the difficulty too high? Adjust the times and patch the code for next week.

[PRESS START TO CONTINUE]

Chapter 8: Resource Management

You have picked your class. You have optimized your UI. You are crushing your Dailies.

But now you are hitting a wall. You are capped.

In every MMO there is a limit to what a solo player can achieve. You can grind mobs and do daily quests alone, but you cannot enter the High-Level Raids. You cannot kill the endgame bosses. You cannot scale.

To unlock the next tier of success you need to stop playing solo and start **Building Your Guild.**

This is the hardest transition for a Solopreneur. You are used to having 100% control. You are used to being the Tank, DPS, and Healer. But if you want to build an empire you have to trust other people with the controller.

The LFG (Looking For Group) Nightmare

If you have ever used an LFG (Looking For Group) tool in *Destiny* or *World of Warcraft*, you know the horror. You invite random people. They lie about their gear score. They don't know the mechanics. They quit after one wipe.

Hiring employees or finding business partners is exactly the same.

Most people hire based on a resume (Gear Score). They see a degree or a flashy previous job title and think "This person is a Pro."

I don't care about your resume. I care about your mechanics. I care about how you communicate when we are wiping in a boss fight.

The "Kick" List (Red Flags)

Over years of leading raids in *Destiny* and coaching high-performance teams in the real world, I have developed a zero-tolerance policy for toxic players.

If I see these Red Flags, I won't hire you. If I see them after I hire you, I kick you from the party.

1. The "Know-It-All" (Arrogance) These are the players who think they are better than the Raid Leader. They join your business and immediately act like they know more than you do, but without the results to back it up.

- ***The Gaming Equivalent:*** The guy who sprints ahead, pulls the boss before the team is ready, dies immediately, and then blames the Healer.

- ***The Fix:*** Immediate kick. Arrogance destroys team cohesion.

2. The Role Refuser These people agree to a job description (the Role) but then refuse to do it. You hired them to Tank (Operations), but they keep trying to DPS (give marketing ideas).

- ***The Gaming Equivalent:*** The player who agrees to hold the relic or shoot the glowing orb, but then decides they'd rather just kill add's, causing a team wipe.

- ***The Reality:*** If you agree to a role, do the role. If you want to play a different class, go join a different guild or ask before jumping into something outside your role.

3. The Comm-less Player (Refusal to Communicate) I don't mean people who don't understand. I mean people who refuse to talk it out when it is needed. They go silent. They hide mistakes.

- ***The Gaming Equivalent:*** The player with no microphone who refuses to type in chat. You don't know if they are ready or if they know the mechanic.

- ***The Reality:*** Silence is death. If I can't communicate with you, I can't trust you.

4. The "It Was Lag" Guy (Zero Responsibility) They take no responsibility for a failed attempt. It is always the market, the software, the customer, or the "lag."

- ***The Gaming Equivalent:*** The guy who falls off the map and blames the physics engine every single time.

- **The Reality:** I can work with someone who says, "My bad, I messed up." I cannot work with someone who says, "The controller broke."

5. The Askhole (Ask-Hole) They ask for help but don't want to listen. They ask for your advice, you give it to them, and they ignore it. Then they come back and ask again.

- **The Gaming Equivalent:** "How do I beat this boss?" You tell them exactly where to stand. They stand somewhere else. They die. "Why did I die?"

6. The Fragile Ego (Can't Take Criticism) They view feedback as a personal attack. You tell them their code is buggy or their sales script is weak, and they have an emotional breakdown or get defensive.

- **The Gaming Equivalent:** You tell a guy to switch weapons because his DPS is low, and he rage-quits the party.

- **The Reality:** If you can't take criticism, you can't level up.

7. The Karen (The Griefer) They exist solely to drag everyone down. They blame you when they can't do their role. They think they are right despite all evidence to the contrary.

- ***The Gaming Equivalent:*** The toxic player who screams at the team after *they* caused the wipe.

- ***The Reality:*** These are energy vampires. They will drain your Mana bar faster than any boss. Remove them immediately.

8. The "Yes Man" (The Sycophant) This is a hidden killer. I won't go for people who tell me what they think I want to hear. They smile and nod when I have a bad idea.

- ***The Gaming Equivalent:*** The teammate who says "Yeah I know the mechanics" when they clearly don't, just to get into the group.

- ***The Reality:*** I need honest feedback. If I am walking off a cliff, I need a team member who will grab me, not one who claps.

SIDE QUEST:
THE RECRUITMENT PROTOCOL

Quest Giver: The Raid Leader
Difficulty: Critical (High Stakes)
XP Reward: +100 Leadership, +1 Party Stability
Unlock: The "Ban Hammer" Ability

Objective: Building a Guild is dangerous. One toxic player can wipe the entire party. Your mission is to ignore the "Gear Score" (Resume) and inspect the "Base Stats" (Character) before you send an invite.

Mission Parameters:

1. Engage Passive Perception (The Vibe Check) You cannot quantify this on a spreadsheet, but your brain's anti-cheat software picks it up.

- **The Action:** In your next meeting or interview, stop listening to *what* they say and focus on *how* they say it.

- **The Lag Check:** Is there a delay in their answers? Is there a lack of eye contact? Do you feel a knot in your stomach?

- **The Rule:** If the Vibe is off, the answer is **NO**. Do not try to debug a bad personality.

2. Inspect Base Stats (Honesty & Loyalty) Skills (DPS/Healing) can be taught. You can power-level someone in Excel or AI. You cannot patch their source code.

- **The Test:** Ask them about a time they failed.

    - *If they own it:* High Honesty. (Keep).

    - *If they blame the "lag," the "controller," or their old boss:* Low Honesty. (Kick).

- **The Reality:** You either spawn with Honesty and Loyalty, or you don't. Do not hire someone hoping you can mod them later.

3. The Party Wipe Calculation Before you hire, calculate the damage cap.

- **The Simulation:** Imagine this person turns toxic in 3 months. Can they crash the server? Can they steal the client list? Can they ruin the culture?

- **The Decision:** A bad hire is not just a waste of gold; it is a Party Wipe. It is better to run a 2-man dungeon with someone you trust than a 40-man raid with people looking for the exit.

4. The Kick Command If you have already hired someone who is showing Red Flags (The "Karen," The "Role Refuser," or The "Liar"):

- **The Action:** Initiate the Kick Command immediately.

- **The Mindset:** You are not "being mean." You are protecting the other players in your guild.

Status Update: Guard the gate. A small elite squad will always beat a massive, disorganized mob.

[PRESS START TO CONTINUE]

Chapter 9: The Tech Tree

In strategy games like *Civilization* or RPGs like *Skyrim*, you have a "Tech Tree."

You start with basic skills like "Mining" or "Archery." As you gain XP, you spend points to unlock advanced skills. You cannot unlock "Nuclear Fission" until you have unlocked "Physics."

In the real world, skills function exactly the same way. But the education system tries to trick you. They try to sell you the entire Tech Tree for $50,000 upfront before you have even played the tutorial.

To stop being an NPC, you need to take control of your own skill acquisition. You need to become a self-learning machine.

Paid DLC vs. Free-to-Play (The Degree Dilemma)

When I wanted to learn Full Stack Development, I was lost. I didn't know where to start. I wanted a structured approach so I paid nearly £8,000 for a degree.

Looking back, I ask myself: Was it worth it?

The answer is yes and no.

The "No": Could I have learned the skills for free? Absolutely. There are thousands of tutorials, walkthroughs, and documentation files available for zero cost. If you are willing to bootstrap, you can learn just as fast as a student by grinding YouTube and Stack Overflow. The information is not locked behind a paywall anymore.

The "Yes": The money didn't buy me "secrets." It bought me **Structure** and **Community**. It gave me access to a guild of like-minded individuals. That network was priceless.

The Lesson: If you need a map, pay for the course. If you are willing to explore the map yourself, learn for free. Neither path guarantees you a job. Only your skills do that.

Thrown to the Wolves (The Gamer Method)

How does a gamer learn a new game?

Do we read the 50-page instruction manual before we press Start? No. We press Start. We get thrown into the level. We try to jump over a pit. We fall. We die. We respawn. We will try again.

We learn on the fly.

This is called **Active Recall**.

Schools teach you "*Just-in-Case*" information. They teach you facts you *might* need in ten years. Gamers use "*Just-in-Time*" learning. We learn the mechanic because we need to beat the boss *right now*.

For my businesses, I stopped trying to learn everything upfront. I let myself be thrown to the wolves. I fail more times than I succeed. I am not afraid to make an utter fool of myself because I learn so much more from failure than from theory.

In a game, "Game Over" just means "Try Again." In business, a failed project is just data on how to do it better next time.

The Daily XP Cap

You cannot go from Level 1 to Level 60 in one day. If you try to cram 12 hours of learning into one session, your brain will crash.

I treat every day as a learning day. My rule is simple: **Learn one thing each day.**

It doesn't matter how big or small it is.

- Maybe it's a new keyboard shortcut.

- Maybe it's how to file a specific tax form.

- Maybe it's a new marketing psychological trigger.

Forget about "learning fast" or "learning slow." Learn at your own pace. The goal is to keep the brain functioning. Neuroplasticity is real. If you stop learning, your account starts to decay. You become obsolete.

Strategy Guides (Books)

The one thing I regret is not using "Strategy Guides" sooner.

For years, I tried to figure everything out by trial and error. I wish I had read more books like the one you are holding right now.

A non-fiction book is literally a Strategy Guide written by a player who has already beaten the level. They have put 10+ years of grinding into 100+ pages. Reading it is a cheat code. It unlocks potential that would take you a decade or more to find on your own.

SIDE QUEST: INITIALIZE SKILL DOWNLOAD

Quest Giver: The Architect
Difficulty: Variable (Depends on your Gold/Time balance)
XP Reward: +1 Skill Point, +50 Intelligence
Unlock: The "Autodidact" Achievement

Objective: The University system sells you a generic pre-built character. To build a custom build that dominates the meta, you must manually install the specific skills required for your Class.

Mission Parameters:

1. Select the Active Ability Refer back to your Class Audit (Chapter 5). What is the one skill that is currently bottlenecking your progress?

- *If Tank:* QuickBooks, Notion, Tax Law.

- *If DPS:* Copywriting, Facebook Ads, Public Speaking.

- *If Crafter:* Python, Video Editing, 3D Design.

- **The Rule:** Pick **ONE**. You cannot download five large files at once without crashing the system.

2. Select the Download Speed (Choose Your Mode) You have two currencies: **Time** or **Gold**. You must spend one to save the other.

- **Mode A: Free-to-Play (F2P)**

    - *Source:* YouTube, Documentation, Reddit, Discord.

    - *Cost:* $0 Gold / High Time Requirement.

    - *Pro:* Accessible immediately.

    - *Con:* You have to filter through "trash mobs" (bad advice) to find the loot.

- **Mode B: Paid DLC (Pay-to-Win)**

    - *Source:* Bootcamps, Specific Courses, 1-on-1 Coaching.

    - *Cost:* High Gold / Low Time Requirement.

    - *Pro:* Fast Travel. It gives you the structure immediately.

    - *Con:* Expensive.

3. Execute the Daily Patch You cannot install the whole skill in one night. You must install it in packets.

- **The Grind:** Commit to learning **one single mechanic** of that skill every day.

    - *Day 1:* How to open the software.

    - *Day 2:* How to write one line of code.

    - *Day 3:* How to render a file.

- **The Streak:** Do not break the chain. 30 days of small patches equals a massive system upgrade.

Status Update: Do not wait for a professor to give you permission to learn. The server is open. The files are hosted. Start the download.

[PRESS START TO CONTINUE]

PART IV: MULTIPLAYER MODE

Chapter 10: Building Your Guild

In every online game there is a specific type of player known as a Griefer or a Troll.

They don't play the objective. They don't care about winning. Their only goal is to make you miserable. They spam the chat. They block doorways. They try to get a reaction out of you.

In business we call them "Karens," haters, or toxic customers.

If you are going to be a Main Character you need to accept a hard truth. You will attract hate. You cannot be visible without drawing Aggro. The only people who have zero haters are the NPCs who never leave the house.

The Door-to-Door Speedrun

I learned how to handle these mobs in the trenches. I used to go door-to-door selling charity subscriptions.

This is the hardest difficulty setting for sales. You are interrupting people in their own homes. In their defense, strangers showing up at the door is often annoying or scary. But the reaction I got was often pure venom.

People would open the door and immediately tell me to F-off.

Most people would crumble. They would try to argue or they would let it ruin their day.

I used a different tactic. I called it the "Friendly Speedrun."

The moment they got angry I would smile and say "Sorry for wasting your time, have a nice day!"

And then I would immediately walk away.

I didn't wait for a response. I didn't wait for them to slam the door. I was halfway to the next house before they finished processing the sentence.

One time the biggest Karen I ever met was so shocked by this that she actually called out after me. She wanted to know why I rang the bell. She was confused because I broke her script. She wanted a fight and I gave her a polite exit.

But I didn't turn back. I put her in the rear view.

Don't Waste Mana on NPCs

Why did I walk away so fast?

Because time is a resource. In sales and business your Mana is your emotional energy. If I spent 10 minutes arguing with that woman I would have lost the energy to pitch to the next house.

She was an NPC. Her dialogue was set to "Hostile." There was no quest there. No loot. No XP.

Why waste my stats on an encounter that drops nothing?

I see so many business owners getting into keyboard wars in the comment section. They write five-paragraph essays defending themselves against a troll on Twitter.

You are losing. Even if you win the argument you lost the time. You fed the troll.

The Entitlement Virus

I hate entitlement more than anything.

We live in a society where people have been brought up to expect the world to cater to them. They believe the customer is always right even when the customer is acting like a toddler.

While you should do your best to serve people it does not mean giving up your values. It does not mean letting people abuse you or your staff.

If a client demands you work for free or speaks to you like dirt you don't need to please them. You need to fire them.

Protect your boundaries. A Main Character has a code of honor. An NPC has a script of compliance.

Bad Reviews are Just Patch Notes

You will eventually get a bad review. It might be fair or it might be unhinged.

When it happens don't panic. Reframing is key.

Think of a bad review as a Bug Report. Read it. Is there truth in it? Did you actually mess up the shipping? Did the product break?

If yes then thank them. They just gave you free data on how to fix your business. Use it to patch the game and make it better.

If no and they are just being hateful then ignore it. It is just noise.

Hate is a Metric of Success

In gaming the more damage you do the more "Aggro" you pull. The boss focuses on the player doing the most DPS.

Life works the same way.

If you are getting hate it usually means you are doing something right. It means you are disrupting the status quo. It means you are visible.

If everyone agrees with you then you aren't saying anything important. If nobody is criticizing you then nobody knows who you are.

More hate often shows you are on the right path to change.

Don't let the trolls slow down your speedrun. Smile. Apologize for their bad mood. And keep walking to the next door.

SIDE QUEST:
AGGRO MANAGEMENT TRAINING

Quest Giver: The Veteran Tank
Difficulty: Hard (Requires suppressing the ego)
XP Reward: +100 Emotional Armor, +50 Mana Conservation
Unlock: The "Teflon Mindset" Perk

Objective: You are generating Aggro. This is a good sign—it means your DPS is high. However, if you let the mobs surround you, you will die. Your mission is to practice **Strategic Disengagement**.

Mission Parameters:

1. The "Wall of Text" Ban Check your recent combat logs (Social Media comments, Emails, Discord). Find a Troll or a "Karen."

- **The Impulse:** You want to write a 500-word defense explaining why they are wrong.

- **The Restriction:** You are banned from using the "Reply" button.

- **The Action:** Delete the comment. Block the user. Or simply leave it there as a trophy of your visibility.

- **The Logic:** Do not spend 50 Mana on a creature that drops 0 Loot.

2. Execute the Friendly Speedrun The next time you encounter a hostile NPC in real life (a rude client, an angry family member, a toxic stranger):

- **Equip the Script:** *"I can see you are upset. I'm going to go now. Have a nice day."*

- **The Mechanic:** Deliver the line with a smile. Turn 180 degrees. Walk away.

- **The Test:** Do not look back. If they yell after you, keep walking. You are speedrunning to the next objective; they are stuck in the level.

3. Analyze the Patch Notes Take your last piece of criticism (a bad review or a mean comment).

- **The Binary Choice:**

  - *Is it a Bug Report?* (e.g., "The link is broken," "The shirt shrank.") -> **Fix it.** Thank them.

  - *Is it Noise?* (e.g., "You suck," "Who do you think you are?") -> **Discard it.**

- **The Goal:** Separate the signal from the static.

Status Update: If you have zero haters, you are still in the tutorial. If you have haters, congratulations. You have entered the endgame. Keep your shield up and keep moving.

[PRESS START TO CONTINUE]

Chapter 11: Don't Feed the Trolls

In gaming, a Boss Battle tests everything you have learned so far. It tests your gear, your skills, and your nerves.

In business, the first true Raid Boss isn't a competitor. It isn't a market crash.

It is **The System itself.**

It is the paperwork. It is the legal structure. It is the overwhelming realization that you have no idea what you are doing and one wrong move could cost you everything.

Phase 1: The Bureaucracy Dungeon

For me, the single most crisis-inducing moment wasn't losing money. It was launching my business from a legal perspective.

I was staring at the UK Law requirements like a player staring at a raid mechanic they didn't understand. Sole Proprietor? Limited Company? VAT thresholds?

I didn't know where to start. So I used the gamer strategy: **I just pressed Start.**

I started as a Sole Proprietor for the first six months. I played the early levels on "Easy Mode" while I built the brand. But then I hit the privacy mechanic.

The "Doxing" Mechanic

As a gamer, I value privacy. The idea of my home address being plastered on a public database for any bad actor to find was a dealbreaker. I didn't want to dox myself just to sell t-shirts.

This is where I realized I needed to "Pay-to-Win" the bureaucracy.

I transitioned to a Limited Company (LTD), but instead of using my home address, I used a service called **1st Formations**.

For about £90, they set it all up. They provided a registered office address in London. It was cheaper than a PO Box and it gave me a massive buff: **Anonymity.** My personal address stayed private. My family stayed safe.

Just when I thought I had beaten the boss, a new add spawned.

I realized I was collecting user data (emails, shipping info). That triggered the **ICO (Information Commissioner's Office)** requirement. Another £47 fee.

These hidden fees and rules are the "invisible mechanics" of business. You don't see them coming, but if you ignore them, they can wipe your party.

The Lesson: Don't try to tank the legal damage yourself. Use services (Mercenaries) to handle the compliance so you can focus on the game.

Phase 2: The Overwhelm Loop

I am going to be honest with you. I am in a forever loop of constantly feeling overwhelmed.

There is so much to learn about brand identity. There are so many paths to take. The clothing industry is "Hard Mode." It is low margin, high competition, and financially punishing if you get it wrong.

But here is the secret: **There is no right path.**

This is an open-world RPG being written in real-time. You are the developer and the player. You make a mistake (glitch), you patch it (learn), and you keep playing.

If you are waiting for the feeling of overwhelm to go away, you will be waiting forever. The overwhelm just means you are playing at a high level.

Phase 3: The "New Game+" Strategy

If I could respawn and start my clothing brand over today with the knowledge I have now, I would play the meta completely differently.

The Old Strat (RNG): I designed shirts, paid for stock, and hoped people liked them. This is gambling. This is relying on the Random Number Generator.

The New Strat (Validation): I would create one design a week. I would press it on a single shirt. I would wear it in public. I would post it online.

I would treat it like a "Pre-Order" quest. I wouldn't manufacture a single batch until I had 100+ orders confirmed.

Why? because knowing what a consumer wants is the hardest mechanic in the game.

- If you guess? You lose money on dead stock.

- If you validate? You have a guaranteed win.

Unless you have a massive following of loyal fans who will buy anything you drop, do not play the RNG game. Test the market.

Surviving the Wipe

You will make mistakes. You will miss a tax deadline. You will launch a product that gets zero sales.

In a game, when you wipe on a boss, you don't snap the disc in half. You look at the combat log. You see what killed you. And you go again.

The only true "Game Over" is when you quit. Everything else is just a checkpoint restart.

SIDE QUEST: OPERATION SYSTEM OVERRIDE

Quest Giver: The Strategist

Difficulty: Variable (Depends on your willingness to spend Gold vs. Time)

XP Reward: +100 Legal Defense, +200 Market Insight

Unlock: The "Merchant" Class

Objective: You are about to enter a high-level zone. If you go in naked, the "Bureaucracy Boss" will one-shot you. Your mission is to equip the correct armor (Legal Structure) and disable the RNG mechanics (Validation) before you spend your life savings.

Mission Parameters:

1. Equip the Privacy Shield (Pay-to-Win) Do not try to be a lawyer. You are not specced for that.

- **The Audit:** Are you holding back because you don't understand the paperwork?

- **The Action:** Find your "Mercenary."

    - *In the UK:* Look at services like 1st Formations.

    - *In the US:* Look at ZenBusiness or Incfile.

- **The Check:** Will this service hide your home address? If yes, bookmark it. You now know exactly how much Gold you need to buy "Peace of Mind." Stop worrying about the law; just save the fee to pay the mercenary.

2. Disable RNG (The Validation Protocol) You are forbidden from buying inventory. You are forbidden from building the full app.

- **The Task:** Create a "Ghost Item."

- Mock up your product (digital design, landing page, or just a really good description).

- **The Test:** Put it in front of 10 people (or run $20 of ads). Ask them to buy it *now* as a pre-order.

- **The Result:**

  - *If nobody buys:* You just saved thousands of dollars. **Mission Success.**

  - *If people buy:* You have unlocked "Guaranteed Loot." Now you can build it.

3. The Checkpoint Save You will eventually mess up. You will miss a form. You will get a Scary Letter from the government.

- **The Protocol:** When the "Fear Debuff" hits you, do not Rage Quit.

- **The Mantra:** Say this out loud: *"This is not a Game Over. This is just a puzzle mechanic. I will find the walkthrough."*

Status Update: The System is designed to be intimidating. It is a graphical illusion. Pay the fee. Validate the loot. Ignore the noise.

[PRESS START TO CONTINUE]

Chapter 12: Understanding "The Meta"

In competitive gaming the "Meta" stands for the **Most Effective Tactic Available**.

It is the loadout, the strategy, or the character build that is currently dominating the game. But every gamer knows the golden rule of the Meta: **It always changes.**

The developers release a patch. They "nerf" the weapon you loved. They "buff" a class you hate. They change the map.

If you refuse to adapt to the new patch you will lose. You can be the most skilled player in the world but if you are using a strategy from three patches ago you will get destroyed by a noob using the current Meta.

Business works exactly the same way. The market is the game. The "Developers" are the tech giants, the economy, and the culture.

Reading the Patch Notes (Market Trends)

Most NPCs ignore the patch notes. They get comfortable. They find a way to make money or do a job and they think it will last forever.

Then the patch drops.

- **The Patch:** AI enters the chat.

- **The Patch:** TikTok changes the algorithm to favor long videos over short ones.

- **The Patch:** A recession hits and luxury spending drops.

The NPC complains. They say "The game is broken" or "It's not fair."

The Player reads the patch notes. They ask "Okay, how do I exploit this?"

When I saw AI starting to rise I didn't panic about it taking my job. I equipped it. I used it to speed up my workflow by 80%. I turned a threat into a buff.

You need to constantly review what strategies are obsolete. If you are still trying to grow a business using strategies from 2015 you are playing on a dead server.

Don't Build on Rented Servers

The biggest mistake I see new players make is building their entire empire on rented land.

They build a massive following on Instagram, TikTok, or Amazon. They think they are winning because the follower count is high.

But they don't own the server.

At any moment the Admin (Zuckerberg, Musk, Bezos) can shut down the server. They can ban your account.

They can change the algorithm so nobody sees your posts.

If your business lives entirely on social media you do not have a business. You have a profile on someone else's website.

Owning the Save File (Data Ownership)

This is why I took the time to register with the ICO and pay the data protection fees.

I want to own the "Save File."

In business the Save File is your **Email List** and your **Customer Data**.

- Social Media is for **Discovery** (finding people).

- Email/SMS is for **Retention** (owning the relationship).

If Instagram shuts down tomorrow I still have a list of customers I can email directly. I can still sell t-shirts. I can still offer coaching.

If you are not moving your followers from "Rented Land" (Social Media) to "Owned Land" (Email List), you are one server crash away from Game Over.

The Pivot (Changing Class)

Sometimes the Meta shifts so hard that your current Class becomes unplayable.

In gaming, this is when you "Re-roll." You create a new character. In business, this is called a **Pivot**.

Maybe you started a streetwear brand but you realize the "Meta" has shifted to sustainable fabrics. You pivot. Maybe you started as a coder but AI is writing the code now. You pivot to becoming a "Prompt Engineer" or a "Systems Architect."

Don't be sentimental about your build.

If I notice that a specific t-shirt design isn't selling I don't force it. I don't try to convince the market they are wrong. I accept the data. I drop the design. I make a new one.

Stubbornness is not a virtue in a changing game. Agility is.

Avoiding Server Shutdown

You need to diversify your spawn points.

If you rely on one traffic source you are fragile. If you rely on one client for 90% of your income you are fragile. If you rely on one product you are fragile.

The goal of the Endgame is to build a system that can survive a server shutdown. You want to be decentralized. You want to have multiple ways to win.

The Meta will change. The patch will drop. The question is will you be the player complaining in the forums or the player dominating the leaderboard with the new gear?

This Side Quest forces the reader to face the uncomfortable truth about their business stability and adapt to the changing rules of the game (The Meta).

SIDE QUEST: THE META-GAME ANALYSIS

Quest Giver: The Meta Analyst
Difficulty: Strategic (Requires future-proofing)
XP Reward: +100 Stability, +50 Adaptability
Unlock: The "Server Admin" Status

Objective: The game has been patched. The rules have changed. If you are still playing with a Season 1 build in Season 10, you will get crushed. Your mission is to audit your loadout and ensure you aren't building your castle on temporary servers.

Mission Parameters:

1. The Server Stability Test (Rented vs. Owned) List every source where you currently gather loot (customers/attention).

- **Rented Servers (Third-Party):** Instagram, TikTok, LinkedIn, YouTube, Amazon.

- **Local Save Files (Owned):** Email List, Phone Numbers, Your Website.

- **The Simulation:** Imagine a "Server Wipe." If Instagram and TikTok deleted your account today, does your business die?

- ○ *If Yes:* Your Main Quest is now urgent: **Migrate the user base.** Create a "Lead Magnet" (Free Guide/Discount) to move followers from Rented Land to your Email List immediately.

2. Inspect the Patch Notes (Trend Check) Look at the current "Meta" of your industry. What is the new "Overpowered Weapon" everyone is talking about? (e.g., AI, Short-Form Video, Sustainability).

- **The Binary Choice:**

  - ○ *Are you ignoring it?* (You will be nerfed).

  - ○ *Are you equipping it?* (You will be buffed).

- **The Task:** Spend **one hour** this weekend researching the biggest technological threat to your industry. Do not fear it. Figure out how to put it in your inventory.

3. Execute the Kill Switch (Inventory Management) Look at your product line or service list. Identify the "Dead Item." The thing that hasn't sold in 6 months but you keep trying to revive.

- **The Action:** Stop wasting mana on resurrection spells.

- **The Command: DELETE.** Remove it from the store. Stop talking about it.

- **The Benefit:** You just freed up bandwidth to build something that actually fits the current Meta.

Status Update: The game evolves. If you stay static, you become glitchy legacy code. Update your build. Own your data. Clear the cache.

[PRESS START TO CONTINUE]

PART V: ENDGAME

Chapter 13: The Boss Battle

In the early game, you fight mobs. They are annoying, but manageable. In the mid-game, you fight elites. They hit harder, but you have better gear. In the Endgame, you fight **Bosses**.

A Boss Battle is different. It has mechanics that can wipe your entire party in one hit. It requires focus, preparation, and emotional control.

In business, the Boss Battle looks like a lawsuit, a massive launch day, or a complete mental breakdown from overwhelm.

The Crisis Checklist
(When the Screen Flashes Red)

When I was setting up my business, I hit a mechanic I wasn't prepared for: The Legal System.

I was staring at requirements for Sole Proprietorship vs Limited Company. I was worried about doxing myself by putting my home address on public records. Then I got hit with the ICO (Information Commissioner's Office) data protection fees.

I felt the panic setting in. This is the moment most players **Rage Quit**. They see a government form they don't understand, and they freeze.

To survive a crisis, you need a **Crisis Checklist**. This is the tactical framework I use when the screen flashes red:

1. **Pause the Game (Stop the Bleeding):** Do not make rash decisions when you are panicked. If you receive a scary letter or an angry email, do nothing for 60 minutes. Let the adrenaline fade.

2. **Identify the Mechanic:** What is actually happening? Is it a "wipe mechanic" (I'm going to jail) or just a "damage mechanic" (I have to pay a £47 fee)? Usually, it's just a fee.

3. **Call in a Mercenary:** I didn't try to become a lawyer. I hired **1st Formations**. I paid ~£90. I used their address to protect my privacy. I paid the "Tank" to take the damage for me.

4. **Execute the Mechanic:** Do the paperwork. Pay the fine. Send the apology email. Do it without emotion.

The Massive Launch Day (Avoiding RNG)

The other type of Boss Battle is the **Product Launch**.

This is high-stress, high-reward. Most people play this wrong. They play it like a slot machine. They design a product, buy 500 units of stock, and "hope" people buy it.

That is relying on RNG (Random Number Generation). In a Boss fight, RNG gets you killed.

If I could restart my clothing brand today, I would use the **Validation Strat**:

1. **The Tease:** Create one design.

2. **The Test:** Press it on a single shirt. Wear it. Post it.

3. **The Pre-Order:** Set up a wishlist or a pre-order page.

4. **The Condition:** Do not manufacture a single unit until you have 100+ orders.

If you don't get 100 orders, you won't "fail." You just avoided a team wipe. You saved the money you would have wasted on dead stock.

You don't run into the Boss room blindly. You check if you have the DPS (Demand) first.

Avoiding the Rage-Quit (Emotional Resilience)

I am going to be honest with you. I am in a forever loop of constantly feeling overwhelmed.

There is always more to learn. Brand identity, marketing, legal compliance. It feels like the Boss has a billion health points and you are chipping away with a toothpick.

This is where many players quit. They feel overwhelmed and assume they are playing the game wrong.

You aren't playing it wrong. That *is* the game.

The overwhelm is simply the sensation of the difficulty curve increasing. When you feel like quitting, you need to remember: **The only true Game Over is when you choose to stop playing.**

Everything else (*a failed launch, a bad review, a lost shipment*) is just a checkpoint restart. You respawn. You try again.

Post-Mortem Analysis (The Combat Log)

After a Boss Battle (*whether you won or lost*) you must look at the data.

In *World of Warcraft*, after a wipe, we look at the "Combat Log." We see exactly what killed us. "Oh, the Tank didn't use a shield wall at 20% health."

In business, you need to do a **Post-Mortem Analysis**.

- **If you succeeded:** Why? Was it the Facebook ad? Was it the influencer? Was it just luck? If you don't know why you won, you can't repeat it.

- **If you failed:** Why? Was the price too high? Was the website slow? Did the design suck?

I see so many people fail a business and say "I guess business isn't for me." No. That's lazy. Look at the logs. Maybe business *is* for you, but you just need to fix one mechanic (e.g., your shipping costs were too high).

You make mistakes. You learn. You do something right. You learn.

It is a personal RPG written in real-time.

SIDE QUEST: THE COMBAT LOG DEBRIEF

Quest Giver: The Data Analyst
Difficulty: Moderate (Requires honesty)
XP Reward: +100 Wisdom, +50 Strategy
Unlock: The "Veteran" Status

Objective: You just finished a Boss Battle (a launch, a crisis, or a major project). Whether you won or wiped, the run is useless if you don't save the data. Your mission is to stop guessing why things happened and look at the code.

Mission Parameters:

1. Open the Console (The Template) Grab a notebook or a blank document. You are going to create a permanent record of this battle. Copy this exact schema:

- **THE EVENT:** (Name the Battle. e.g., Black Friday Sale, Hiring a VA, Launching the new Website).

- **THE OUTCOME:** (Binary choice: **Success** or **Mission Failed**?)

2. Analyze the Damage (The Red Text) List everything that went wrong. Be specific. "It went bad" is not data.

- *Bad Data:* "People didn't buy."

- *Good Data:* "I ran out of stock on Day 2," or " The checkout link returned a 404 error," or "The ad spend was too high for the margin."

3. Analyze the Buffs (The Green Text) List everything that went right. You need to know what to keep.

- *Examples:* "The email subject line had a 40% open rate," "The server held up under traffic," "The customer support script worked."

4. Release the Patch (The Fix) This is the most critical step. Based on the data above, what is the **one rule** you are changing for the next run?

- *The Patch Note:* "Next time, I will order 20% more stock."

- *The Patch Note:* "Next time, I will test the checkout link on mobile before launching."

Status Update: If you win without knowing why, it was luck (RNG). If you lose and learn why, it was progress (XP). Fill out the log. Patch the game. Go again

[PRESS START TO CONTINUE]

Chapter 14: New Game+

In video games, when you beat the final boss and the credits roll, the game isn't always over.

Many games unlock a mode called **New Game+**.

You start the journey over from the beginning, but you keep all your gear, your skills, and your stats. You are overpowered. The enemies are stronger, but you are a god. The goal shifts from "Survival" to "Mastery."

In life, "New Game+" is the phase you enter when you stop worrying about survival (money) and start focusing on significance (legacy).

The Meaning of "Winning"

People ask me what I would do if I "won" the game of capitalism. If I woke up tomorrow with $100 million in the bank, would I retire to a beach and drink margaritas?

No. That sounds like hell.

If I had $100 million tomorrow, the only thing that would change is the *scale* of the help I give. The "payday stress" would disappear. I would buy the homestead or the fixer-upper house my wife and I always wanted. We would document the journey, fix it up, and share what we learned with the world.

But I would never stop working.

If you love what you do, you don't think of it as "work." It is just gameplay.

If you wake up in the morning and dread what you do (*if it starts to feel like "work"*) that is a notification from the system. It means you need to re-evaluate your life. It means you need to plan your exit to the next big idea.

Winning isn't about stopping. It's about playing the game on your own terms.

The Zombie State (Purpose Beyond Money)

We are a tribal species. Love it or hate it, helping others is hardcoded into our DNA

When you ignore this (*when you play the game solely for yourself, hoarding gold and ignoring the other players*) you start to glitch.

The more we avoid our nature to help, the deeper our internal scars become. Eventually, you become like a zombie inside. You treat life with such a light touch that nothing matters. You become unhinged. You do things you regret.

It is like a demon takes your soul and consumes you.

I have watched the world for over 30 years. I have read the history books. The trend is always the same: Hate breeds hate. Love breeds love.

Helping others breaks the cycle of the Zombie. It reconnects you to the server. It reminds you that we are all stuck in this simulation together.

Co-Op Mode (Mentorship)

The highest level of gratification isn't getting a drop of legendary loot. It is helping a low-level player get *their* first legendary drop.

This is **Co-Op Mode**.

I realized that my true purpose wasn't just to make money for myself. It was to help my coworkers reach 6-figure earnings or more. It was to help a stranger in a raid beat a boss they had been stuck on for weeks.

When you mentor or coach someone, you are creating a Legacy System. You are planting trees you will never sit under.

You don't need to be religious to see this truth. Helping others find fulfillment is the ultimate cheat code for your own happiness.

The Final Save Point

You are now standing at the end of the tutorial.

You have the mindset (Red/Blue Pill). You have the class (Tank, DPS, Healer, Crafter). You have the schedule (The Dailies). You have the team (The Guild).

The rest of the map is Fog of War. I can't draw it for you. You have to walk into it.

You will make mistakes. You will be overwhelmed. You will deal with Karens and crashes and crises.

But remember: You are not an NPC. You are not a background character in someone else's story. You have the controller.

FINAL QUEST: INITIALIZE NEW GAME+

Quest Giver: The Main Character (You)
Difficulty: Infinite (The Game Never Ends)
XP Reward: +Legacy Status
Unlocked: Open World Mode

Objective: The Tutorial is complete. You have read the manual. You have checked the map. Now, you must unplug from the simulation and enter the server for real.

Mission Parameters:

1. Save Your Progress (The Reflection) You are standing at the Final Save Point. Look back at the version of you that bought this book.

- **The Audit:** That person was an NPC. They were waiting for permission. They were running a script.

- **The Realization:** You are no longer that person. You have the Class, the Guild, and the Stats. Do not revert to the old save file.

2. Enable Co-Op Mode (Avoid the Zombie State) As you enter the Endgame, do not hoard your loot. The "Zombie State" triggers when you play only for yourself.

- **The Mission:** Find a "Level 1" player in your life—a colleague, a friend, or a stranger stuck on a boss you have already beaten.
- **The Action:** Drop them a health potion. Give them advice. Help them without asking for Gold.
- **The Result:** This is how you build Legacy. This is how you win.

3. The Avatar Synchronization (The Final Oath) There is one final input command required to boot up the new reality.

- **Action:** Put this book down. Stand up. Walk to the nearest mirror.
- **The Command:** Look yourself in the eye. Do not promise to be a millionaire. Do not promise to be famous. Those are just side quests.
- **The Oath:** Promise yourself the only thing that matters: *"I will not live on auto-pilot."*

Status Update: The script is broken. The controller is in your hands.

[PRESS START]

[GAME SAVED]

A NOTE FROM THE DEV

Tutorial Complete.

You now have the map, the manual, and the controller. The rest of the game is open-world, and you are free to explore it solo.

However, if you decide you want to optimize your custom build or need a Raid Leader to help you navigate the endgame, the **Co-Op Server** is open.

There is no pressure to join. The party finder is available only if you are ready to stop soloing and start building your empire.

Https://jhmotiv.shop/coach

Equip Your Character

If you just want to rep the guild during your daily grind, the **Item Shop** is unlocked. Grab a "Failure Fuels Success" hoodie or other high-stat gear to buff your armor against the NPC world.

https://jhmotiv.shop/shop

Follow Us

TikTok

https://www.tiktok.com/@jhmotiv

YouTube

https://www.youtube.com/@JHMotiv/shorts

Instagram

https://www.instagram.com/JHMotiv/

X/Twitter

https://x.com/JHMotiv

Website

https://jhmotiv.shop/

XP Boost

The friends, followers, and lurkers who kept the hype train moving. You all share in this High Score.

QUEST COMPLETED!

Main Objective: Finish the Book Status: [SUCCESS]

REWARDS EARNED:

- *Intelligence: +10*
- *Motivation: +50*
- *New Skill Unlocked: Perspective Shift*

NEW SIDE QUEST AVAILABLE: "The Bard's Tale"

Mission Briefing: Every hero needs a chronicler. Your journey through these pages is complete, but the legend grows only if you share your story. The developers (me) need your feedback to balance the game for future players.

Objective: Send a review, a shoutout, or your honest thoughts to the Guild Hall.

Loot Drop: My eternal gratitude and a spot on the "Legends" list in my heart.

> ACCEPT QUEST HERE <

Support@JHMotiv.shop

Appendix: The Cheatsheet

1. THE MASTER PROTOCOL

A summary of every mechanic, translation, and fix from the book.

NPC Concept	Main Character Translation	Actionable Fix
The Lie of Safety	*Safety is the most expensive thing you can buy.*	*Calculate Survival: Savings ÷ Burn Rate. Acknowledge the trapdoor.*
The NPC Loop	*Playing on a Pacifist Server where the goal is just to survive.*	*Source Code Audit: Track your time. Identify NPC Mode vs. Main Character Mode.*
Input Machine	*Consuming content (Watching, Scrolling, Reading).*	*Hello World Protocol: Create one piece of Output and Publish it today.*

Fear of the 'F'	*Being terrified of failure, feedback, and looking stupid.*	*Combat Log Debrief: Treat failure as free data (Patch Notes).*
Relying on RNG	*Launching a product without market research/validation.*	*Validation Protocol: Do not build until you have pre-orders.*
The Druid Problem	*Trying to do everything (Tank, DPS, Healer) yourself.*	*Class Selection: Identify your "Dump Stat" and hire/outsource for it.*
Default Settings	*Playing life with high friction, low focus, and manual effort.*	*UI Optimization: Automate with AI Macros and batch Admin tasks.*
Intensity	*Working 16 hours straight for 3 days and quitting.*	*Server Rotation: Set a hard daily Log Off Time. Focus on Consistency.*
Rented Server	*Building a business entirely on social media.*	*Server Stability Test: Migrate followers to an Owned Asset (Email List).*

Toxic Guild Member	Hiring based on a resume rather than character.	Recruitment Protocol: Inspect Base Stats (Honesty) over Gear Score (Resume).
Aggro Management	Wasting emotional energy arguing with Trolls/Karens.	Friendly Speedrun: Deliver a polite exit line and Walk Away to conserve Mana.
Tech Tree Lock	Waiting for permission or a degree to learn a skill.	Skill Download: Choose the skill you need "Just-in-Time" and start the daily patch.
The Zombie State	Unfulfilling success; playing only for yourself.	Co-Op Mode: Help a low-level player get their first legendary drop.

2. STAT SHEET TRANSLATION EXAMPLES

How to translate your "useless" gaming/job habits into business assets.

Source Mechanic (The Grind)	High-Level Stat (The Translation)	Monetization (Who Pays?)
Handling screaming customers	Crisis Management & De-escalation	Customer Success Manager / Conflict Coach
Leading 40-man raids	Team Leadership & Operations	Project Management / Corporate Trainer
Grinding a skill to Level 99	Delayed Gratification & Resilience	Solopreneur / Endurance Investor
Cornering the Auction House	Market Analysis & Margin Protection	eCommerce Operator / Niche Consultant

3. TACTICAL TOOLS

THE CRISIS CHECKLIST Use this when the screen flashes red (Legal threats, Crashes, Overwhelm).

- *Pause the Game: Stop the bleed. Do nothing for 60 minutes.*
- *Identify the Mechanic: Is it a fine or a Game Over? (Hint: It's almost always just a fine).*
- *Call in a Mercenary: Pay a service (Accountant, Lawyer) to take the legal damage for you.*
- *Execute the Mechanic: Pay the fine. Fix the bug. Go again.*

THE FINAL OATH:
To be said in front of a mirror.

"I will not live on auto-pilot."

FURTHER DEBUGGING

(Recommended DLC)

You have beaten the main campaign, but the best players never stop optimizing their build. If you want to dive deeper into specific mechanics, here are the Strategy Guides I recommend installing to your hard drive.

1. The "Purpose" Patch

Book: *What's Your Dream? by Simon Squibb*

The Mechanic: Pure Co-Op Mode. Simon breaks down the "help first" mechanics of business. If you are stuck in the "Zombie State" and can't find your mission, this is the map you need. It teaches you that business isn't just about gold; it's about solving problems for other players.

2. The "Pricing & Confidence" Expansion

Book: *The Fearless Business Blueprint by Robin Waite*

The Mechanic: This is for the "Healers" and "Crafters" who are undercharging. Robin explains exactly how to stop trading time for money (the NPC trap) and start charging for value.

Book: *Take Your Shot by Robin Waite*

The Mechanic: A narrative guide on how to stop hesitating at the start screen and actually press play on your goals.

3. The "Script Breaker" Mod

Book: *The Millionaire Fastlane by MJ DeMarco*

The Mechanic: The ultimate guide to understanding why the "Get Rich Slow" script (School > Job > Save > Retire) is a glitched path. DeMarco distinguishes between the "Sidewalk" (NPCs) and the "Fastlane" (Main Characters). A harsh but necessary reality check for your financial stats.

4. The "Internal Enemy" Guide

Book: *The War of Art by Steven Pressfield*

The Mechanic: Pressfield identifies the invisible Raid Boss known as "Resistance." If you find yourself procrastinating or self-sabotaging, this book explains the enemy's attack patterns and how to defeat them. Essential reading for Creative Classes.

5. The "Dev Log" Tutorial

Book: *Show Your Work! by Austin Kleon*

The Mechanic: We talked about the "Hello World Protocol." Kleon's book is the manual on how to document your journey, share your "Dev Logs," and build an audience without being an "expert." It proves that the process is the product.

6. The "Daily Quest" Optimizer

Book: *Atomic Habits by James Clear*

The Mechanic: The definitive guide on how to program your "Dailies." It explains the code behind why we do what we do. If you want to automate your good habits and delete your bad ones (optimize your server rotation), this is the technical manual.

7. The "Hard Mode" Expansion (Resilience)

Book: *Tiny Warriors: Lena and Luca by Ashley Johnson*

The Mechanic: Dealing with RNG (Random Number Generation). Sometimes the game throws you a critical failure you didn't see coming (like a medical crisis). This guide teaches you how to keep your party alive when the difficulty setting gets locked to "Nightmare Mode."

Book: *The Dad Who Didn't Break by Ashley Johnson*

The Mechanic: The "Underdog" Build. If the school system or society tagged you as a "Low Tier" player or wrote you off, this book is the walkthrough on how to ignore those labels, grind your own stats, and prove the Admins wrong.

8. The "Glitch" Diagnostic Tool

Book: *What's Stopping You? by Robert Kelsey*

The Mechanic: Sometimes your character freezes even when you press the button. This book is a deep dive into the source code of your hesitation (Fear of Failure, Imposter Syndrome). It helps you find the texture glitch that is blocking your path and patch it.

[QUESTS COMPLETE]

This book was never the game; it was just the manual you read while the level loaded. Now, the server is live. The future isn't a pre-written script-it's an open world waiting for your input.

The safety rails are down. The sequel to this story won't be written by me; it will be written by you. Pick up the controller and make it a bestseller.

See you in the lobby.

John L Hummel